Please Don't Call Me Collect on Mother's Day

Mary McBride
and
Veronica McBride

Illustrations by Christine Tripp

To Sylvia
wishing
you happiness
and laughter.

Mary McBride

Library of Congress Cataloguing-in-Publication Data

Humor

Copyright @ 1996 by Mary McBride

Library of Congress No. 95-81201

Authors: Mary McBride and Veronica McBride

Illustrator: Christine Tripp

Editor: Helen Duffy

Published by The Brothers Grinn, 439 Eisenhower Avenue, Janesville, WI 53545

About the Authors: Mary McBride has been a gag writer for Phyllis Diller and Joan Rivers, and is one of the busiest and funniest speakers in America. She and her daughter, Veronica, have also written *Grandma Knows Best, But No One Ever Listens! Don't Call Mommy at Work Today Unless the Sitter Runs Away, The Empty Nest Symphony, Grandpa Knows Best, But No One Ever Listens,* and *Take This Book and Call Me in the Morning.*

About the illustrator: Christine Tripp has illustrated the previous McBride books and lives with her husband and four children in Ottawa, Ontario, Canada.

Contents

Foreword

Mothers are all trying to bring up children to become good adults. The process can become stressful, and the best help in relieving the stress is to look at the situation with humor.

This book is amazing in the way it takes up every conceivable situation that a mother could encounter and makes it laughable.

As all of you know, I am into lifts, and *"Please Don't Call Me Collect on Mother's Day"* is one of the greatest lifts a mother can get.

Phyllis Diller

Let The Cravings Begin

You must expect some changes;
Your stomach won't be flat.
Every time the baby kicks
You should not ask, "What's that?!"

Hearing the statement, "Hi, my name's Melissa, and I'm going to be your new baby," at the beginning of pregnancy would help you get through this sometimes uncomfortable time. But imagination has to serve.

Don't let negative thoughts slip into your mind, such as, "There will be another mouth to feed, and in that mouth there will be teeth to straighten."

It helps to keep a happiness facade. Don't tear up when someone asks, "How far along are you?"

You have to expect a little unpleasantness in order to deserve this great gift of a child.

You will be pregnant nine months, 24 hours a day. You can never say, "I'm going on break now."

Everything you eat turns to heartburn. Your body is like a car that is not easy to handle. When you walk by a playground, you're afraid some kid will tackle you and say, "You've got our basketball!" You are filled with motherly instincts you can't act upon, such as, "I know that baby needs burping."

Be creative in announcing your pregnancy .

"Blessed event" is not a misnomer, and therefore you should put some thought into your announcement to the father of the impending baby. DO NOT throw the home pregnancy kit at him!

Here are a few suggestions of novel ways to announce your pregnancy:

Circle van and station wagon ads.

Put seven jars of pickles in the grocery cart.

If your husband is changing channels during the commercial of a baby product, say, "Don't turn."

Give him a picture frame and say, "In nine months you can put this on your desk with a photo of a baby in it."

Make one of the following statements:

"How about cutting back on the garden next spring and putting up a swing set?"

"You know how you always complain that the good movies are on in the middle of the night? Now you'll be able to watch them."

"Don't you think it's about time we started to get some use out of the extension leaves for this table?"

"Wouldn't it be nice to have an excuse to leave a party that is boring?"

Inform the grandparents by mail. Letters can arrive simultaneously, while with phone calls, one set of grandparents will be informed "first."

It is very important that you make an early appointment with an obstetrician. He will keep track of your physical condition and prescribe any necessary medication.

However, there are some facts he may not remember to tell you:

Morning sickness sets in when you get out of bed.

Don't think you can avoid it by sleeping until noon.

Having plastic surgery on your nose will not prevent your baby from having a nose like your original one.

Use beach towels after bathing.

Get an unlisted telephone number to cut down on the number of times you have to struggle out of a chair to answer the phone.

Don't be a clock-watcher at work. You will make your co-workers nervous.

Double knot your shoes when you tie them in the morning.

Eating for two doesn't mean ordering two portions. If you do, at least make one order a child's portion.

There are things you can do to boost your morale during pregnancy:

Go to the zoo and read the sign on the elephant cage that says the gestation period is 45 months.

Shop at the end of the day when the clerks' ankles are also swollen.

If you are pregnant on Thanksgiving, watch the Macy Parade to make yourself feel a little less bloated.

Hope that your child's teacher doesn't have her pupils draw pictures of their mothers at this time.

Who Gave The Mother Goose Night Light?

If duplicates happen,
You should muster a grin.
Say, "Isn't this great?! --
There'll be one for each twin."

Sometime during the last trimester, you will be given a baby shower.

A person who gives you a baby shower is a caring person who is fond of you. She will want to do everything she can to make it as nice as possible.

She would never have a game of guessing the circumference of your stomach, nor point out that the pink and blue match your varicose veins.

The following are a few suggestions for the hostess to help her provide the mostest:

> Ask everyone to wear loose clothing so tiny waists and flat stomachs aren't visible.

> Award a prize to the person who comes up with the longest list of baby sitters.

> Award a prize to the person who comes up with the best tip for parenting. The mother with the most children should be the judge.

> Make assembling the gifts that need assembling a shower game.

> Be sure that no more than two people help the guest of honor out of her chair.

This isn't a comfortable time for you, so there may be some unpleasantness. For example, the gift of a potty chair will make you have to go to the bathroom, and the motion of a baby swing could make you nauseous.

At a baby shower be sure that no more than two people help the guest of honor out of a chair.

However, you should go with the excitement of the event. You are celebrating the dawn of a new life.

The following are some tips to help you enjoy your shower to the utmost:

> If you know the wife of your obstetrician even slightly, ask that she be invited. She always knows where her husband is.

> Ask that the shower be a matinee. Pregnancy causes sleepiness.

> Don't hold up breakable gifts. Pregnancy causes clumsiness.

> You can't bring your own chair to the shower, so be careful where you sit. Remember that you are sitting for two.

> Be enthusiastic about each and every gift -- even the shape-up tape from a skinny friend and the cloth diapers from your mother-in-law.

> If the hostess has action games, offer to officiate.

> Make sure the guests don't mistake your "ooohs" for labor pains.

> Take a picture of the shower cake to show your doctor so he'll be understanding about your weight gain.

If you have another child, arrange to have him out of the house when you come in with all those presents for somebody else.

Misery Is Seeing Your Obstetrician At a Travel Bureau

It's not a good move --
Your doctor may fume
If you have "Call Forwarding"
Put in the delivery room.

Pregnancy is like being served a subpoena. You must appear in the delivery room. It is nine months until you must be there, but the time will eventually come.

When a baby decides to be born, his determination is awesome. You can wait for the perfect moment to tell your husband you're going to have a baby, but you can't wait for the perfect moment to tell him it's on the way.

If your husband is listening to a game on TV or radio, it is not enough that he turn the volume down so he can hear you tell him how far apart your pains are. He must turn it off.

You should get in the car immediately and head for the hospital. You cannot take time to burn your maternity clothes.

There are a few other delays you should not make:

Settling an argument between your children.

Finishing stenciling Disney characters on the nursery wall.

Getting a substitute for yourself in bridge club.

You cannot pre-register at the hospital. You must stop at the desk of the admitting clerk and answer however many questions she deems necessary.

You can only hope the computer isn't "down."

The delivery room will become your world for a few hours. Even being the center of attention does not make it great.

Try to think positive thoughts. The baby will be a joy.

Your stomach will cease being a globe. You will no longer have to check the sturdiness of chairs.

However, there are some negative aspects. You may never have had an unguarded moment before this, but that record will not remain intact during the delivery.

Try to be as composed as possible.

As soon as the delivery is over, your husband will be one of the good guys again, so don't say anything during the labor that you will be sorry for later.

Fortunately, taking off your wedding ring and throwing it at him is not possible due to swollen fingers.

Every ounce of your husband's being will be concentrated on verbally tranquilizing you.

You husband knows enough not to say "Ouch" when you squeeze his hand, but sometimes he chooses other descriptive words.

Here are a few unwise statements from the father-to-be:

> "Have the nurse motion me to come in the room if it's the <u>real</u> thing."

> "I'm taking notes so I can tell you how you can do it better next time."

> "These people want to get out of here. Can't you hurry a little?"

> "Remember -- when you got pregnant you made a commitment to go through with this."

> "Well, you don't want to spend the rest of your life pregnant, do you?"

However, your husband means well. He would bring the dozen roses into the delivery room if he thought someone would have time to find a vase.

When you are told, "the doctor is on the way," you should not expect his arrival to be imminent. You'll probably start to wonder if his car was hijacked.

Sometimes husbands don't understand

The doctor <u>will</u> get there and take care of you and your baby.

Giving birth is the most exciting event that happens to a woman. Therefore, she may be so elated that she does some foolish things.

A few non-no's are:

> Don't bring your baby book into the delivery room.
>
> Don't call the mayor to tell him to change the population sign.
>
> Don't send an announcement to the manager of the Getaway Motel where the baby was conceived.
>
> Don't send an announcement to your obstetrician.

While there is some unpleasantness to giving birth, there are also things for which to be thankful. The obstetrician does not charge by the hour, which would make a long labor more painful.

When the time has come for you to go to the hospital, you should realize this is also a trying time for your husband. You will know your husband is upset if he offers a $500 reward to anyone who finds your suitcase.

Handle The Handle With Care

A plus of giving a name that he hates --
He won't lounge in bed until ten.
He'll get up the first time that you call
'Cuz he won't want that name called again!

Parents bear the responsibility of selecting a name for the child that will not be a handicap to him or her in the future.

Giving a poor name could be considered a form of child abuse.

If you give a name the child hates, he could fail in school because he won't raise his hand in class.

The name seems to be of particular concern to the mother. However, it is a "must" that you let the father contribute to the decision-making. You cannot say to him when he comes to visit you in the hospital, "I thought I would surprise you and name the baby."

In fact, there is a theory that if you let the father name the baby, he will give more help in caring for the child.

Some parents go overboard in making sure they select the proper name. For instance, it isn't necessary to keep in mind the baby's length at birth, so you give a name that is right for a short or tall person.

Often the mother-to-be stops at a book store on her way home from her first visit to the obstetrician and buys *"The Book of Names"* and even asks the clerk, "What's your name?"

However, you are right to put a great deal of thought into this part of being a mother. You must make sure that it is a name that will sound as good at a Congressional roll call as it will at a romantic tryst.

Here are some suggestions that could help you in naming your baby:

Go to a playground and call out the name you are considering. If more than seven children come running, the prospective name is too popular.

13

Name your child after a character in a classic novel, rather than after one in a soap opera.

If you name your daughter after a friend you are fond of, be sure to ask your friend if she likes her name.

It is romantic to name a child something that will remind you of the conception. This may not be easy, but with enough thought it can always be done. For example, name him "Francis Bernard." You can call him F.B. for "Furnace broke."

Give the child a regal name, such as Victoria. It could help her posture.

Make it a goal to have your child put his or her name on a vanity license plate someday.

Here are some naming no-no's:

Don't give a daughter a double name if your last name is hyphenated. She could decide to keep her maiden name, and, if she marries a man with a hyphenated name, this cumbersome name wouldn't fit in any application blanks.

Don't wait until you get to the hospital to choose the name. You are apt to name the baby after any person who makes you more comfortable, no matter how undesirable the name is.

Don't give your son the name of someone you once dated, even if you love the name.

Don't give your son a tough-sounding name such as "Rock." He will think he is expected to play football, and he might not have the ability. He could get hurt.

Don't tell your boss you'll name the baby after him if it's a boy, if you already know it's going to be a girl. He might find out you already knew your child's sex.

14

Giving her an old-fashioned name will not mean that she will have old-fashioned morals.

15

Here is some important name knowledge:

A child doesn't care in the least what a name means.

There is danger in giving an uncommon spelling of a name. People might think you can't spell.

Some names get more attractive with age, such as Hannah. Others do not, such as Tillie.

Giving a child an old-fashioned name won't mean she will have old-fashioned morals.

If your child keeps telling you how much he hates his name, raise his allowance. It might help a little.

The Baby Won't Call The Sitter "Mommy" After an Hour

The first evening out after Baby
Will be far from being top-notch,
If you look less at the face of your hubby,
Than you look at the face of your watch.

Calling a baby-sitter is one of the most important calls you will ever make.

It is vital that you and your husband go out by yourselves for some sociability soon after the baby is born.

The first time you get a sitter and leave your precious baby is bound to be traumatic.

One mother consulted an astrologist to see whether or not it was advisable to go out on a certain date.

Another mother said, "I feel like I'm dumping my baby. He'll think I prefer to be some place else rather than with him."

This is wrong. Your relationship with your baby will be improved. Also, your relationship with your husband will benefit.

While you must be careful in choosing the person to whom you are going to entrust your baby, it's not going to help to ask the employment agency, "Who is your best sitter?"

You wouldn't be relaxed even if you got a pediatrician to sit for your child.

Forgetting the baby will be impossible. A packet of crackers will make you think of giving a cracker to the baby. The napkin will remind you of a diaper.

You will choose a table near a phone rather than one with a view.

You will say, "Whichever location will get quicker service," when the hostess asks, "Smoking or non-smoking?"

New parents can be a little too cautious

Here are some suggestions for the first evening away from your baby:

> Take your time. Eat dinner at a restaurant and go to a movie. Don't pack a sandwich and eat it during the movie.

> Leave the number where you can be reached in a place where the sitter will be sure to see it, such as on the mirror, on the potato chip box, or on the refrigerator.

> Choose a restaurant where there is music, and then you won't hear sirens.

> Go out with another couple so your husband will have someone to talk to while you make calls home.

> If you have tranquilizers in your medicine chest, take one before you leave the house.

Here are some "don'ts" to observe in order to have the pleasant time you should have on your first night out:

> Don't wave good-bye for a prolonged period. The more you wave, the worse you'll feel.

> Don't repair your make-up. When you go into your purse for your compact, you'll come across the baby's pictures.

> Don't make a U-turn and follow an ambulance.

> Don't go home and check the baby during the play's intermission -- especially if you just checked between dinner and going to the theater.

A new mother must be careful not to be too careful. Some examples of excessive caution are:
> Asking the sitter to move in with you the week be-

fore you are going out, so she and the baby will get to know one another.

Warning the sitter about entertaining boyfriends if she is over 60.

Insisting the sitter sit in a straight chair all evening so she doesn't get sleepy.

Checking the sitter's backpack for headphones.

Stepping back into the house right after you leave, and saying, "What's going on here?!" because she turned on TV.

Getting a car phone installed.

Requesting the phone be placed on the card table, if your evening out is to play bridge.

Pretending you hate the movie so you can leave. You could spend a miserable Oscar Night watching the same movie get 10 awards.

Don't Take Pampers Off the Grocery List Just Yet

It's not hard to explain
Why I'm a griper --
He's nearly three
And still goes in his diaper.

Does the sound of Velcro make you nauseous because you've done so much changing? Are you jealous when you see a mother and child walk into a restroom stall, and you are at the changing table?

The most difficult part of raising a child is getting him out of diapers. You will never know the full meaning of the word exasperation until you've tried to get a toddler to do his duty on the potty chair.

A baby sitter who specializes in toilet training could become wealthy.

It is a war, and the child will eventually surrender, but he fights a fierce battle. What child is more interested in going to the bathroom than playing with toys?

With disposable diapers available, mothers today are not in quite the rush they used to be to train. However, when your mother and mother-in-law give training pants for gifts, it is probably time to get on with it.

So you will know that other mothers experience the same difficulties as you do in accomplishing this feat, here are some examples of mothers' statements during toilet training:

"There should be greeting cards that say: CON-GRATULATIONS ON GETTING YOUR CHILD TRAINED."

"I must say, now that he's older, he's more interesting to sit by."

"Well, at least <u>my</u> hips don't seem as big while she's wearing rubber pants over a diaper."

21

Maybe the water from your eyes will do the trick

Here are some tips that could help in this irritating task:

While the child is sitting on the potty chair, sing songs that suggest water, such as, "My Bonnie Lies Over the Ocean," "London Bridge is Falling Down," or "Way Down Upon the Swanee River."

If you have a teenager in the family, it is better to keep the potty chair in the laundry room. A toddler will not stand outside the bathroom, waiting for an hour.

Wear a pager so your child can call you from the sandbox when she has to go.

Stop playing peek-a-boo while changing him.

To make your child tinkle, try crying. The water from your tears could do the trick.

Ask for tips from someone who is buying training pants, or from someone selling a potty chair at a rummage sale.

Keep up enthusiastic praise every time your child goes on the potty chair. Never say, "Big deal!"

Give the baby-sitter a bonus if she brings training in ahead of schedule.

Learn to read body language.

When you and your husband are both home, don't use the "taking every other trip" method. It's too easy to get mixed up.

Your son should start using the toilet when he starts carrying a newspaper into the bathroom.

Have the diaper service pick up and deliver at your mother's house if your child is embarrassingly old to be "untrained."

An "untrained child" is the best contraceptive there is.

Dictionary of a Mad Mother

In describing your emotions,
It's hard to find words that fit.
But when you do, all mothers
Join you, and say, "That's it!"

Emotions commonly experienced by mothers are misery, wishful thinking, and desperation.

The following situations define these emotions:

Misery is seeing your child get out the crackers as you are putting away the vacuum.

Misery is discovering that it is a contact lens and not a Rice Krispie that you stepped on.

Misery is having your daughter suddenly padlock her diary.

Misery is having to call your son at a friend's house to ask him a computer question.

Misery is having the department store elevator get stuck when taking your kids to the restroom.

Misery is having your child ineligible for kindergarten by one day.

Misery is having the power go off as your daughter starts to blow dry her hair for a date.

Misery is having the boy with whom your son shares apartment expenses at college be his brother.

Misery is typing your child's absence excuse as the school bus comes in sight, and finding your fingers were on the wrong keys.

Misery is having your child eat so much of the batter that you can bake only one cupcake.

A vacuumed rug is short-lived

Misery is cleaning your son's room and finding four books on hang gliding.

Misery is being out of Band-Aids when your child skins his knee and your mother-in-law is visiting.

Misery is having your child break the ribbon that was supposed to be cut by the mayor.

Misery is having your son laugh at his brother's new jacket.

Wishful thinking is having your chid eat a double dip cone, and not getting any ice cream on her clothes.

Wishful thinking is having your son wait until his 21st birthday to drive.

Wishful thinking is having your son sort his dirty clothes.

Wishful thinking is having your daughter's friends practice her words with her before the spelling bee.

Wishful thinking is having your child prefer the cheapest tennis shoes.

Wishful thinking is being able to wear the dress your husband bought you as a gift to wear when bringing the baby home from the hospital.

Desperation is sending an 1873 silver dollar with your child for lunch money.

Desperation is using a pipe cleaner for a shoe lace.

Desperation is taking down your wet laundry so your daughter can have a jump rope.

Desperation is packing your son's lunch in a 30-gallon garbage bag.

Desperation is asking the librarian to meet you at the library after closing hours so your son can get the book he needs.

Desperation is waiting all night in front of the church rummage sale so you can buy back your daughter's blouse that you donated.

In Sickness and in Health, You Must Take Your Child to a Pediatrician

Before you say, "He's got tremors,"
His whole body seems to shake,
Check his Rock 'n Roll music;
That could cause the earth to quake!

You can't give your child protection against bullies, but you can provide him with protection against whooping cough, diphtheria, measles, and polio.

You should have a close relationship with a pediatrician.

It is important that your child like his doctor. However, you shouldn't go so far as to ask your pediatrician to come over to the house and play a Nintendo game with your son before the appointment. Just tell your son how great the doctor is.

To a mother, every complaint is a symptom of a fatal disease. She must be careful not to over-dramatize the problem. For example, don't say, "He has night sweats," because he gets hot tussling with his dog before he goes to bed.

You must realize that children will be exposed to germs and will get sick at one time or another. Nothing can prevent this. Don't give a smaller piece of birthday cake and a smaller dish of ice cream to the kid who gave your kid the flu.

Accidents happen and happen and happen. Mothers aren't judged by the number of stitches and casts their kids get.

A kid is moving every minute, so the chances of his falling, getting cut, or bumping into something are greater than that of an adult who is often sedentary.

It would be nice if doctors ran summer sales on stitches, because children get hurt more when they are out of school.

Feed your child healthy food before his appointment with his pediatrician

Here are some do's and dont's regarding your child's and health:

Don't waste time finding out how the accident happened.

Don't tell yourself his cough is deep because his voice is changing.

The doctor does not want interference from you. Be careful he doesn't say, "Honey, you open your mouth, and, "Mother, you close yours."

Give your child a thorough bath before seeing the doctor. It is embarrassing when the alcohol-moistened cotton turns black.

Feed your child healthy food before his clinic appointment. If the doctor asks him what he had for lunch you want to seem like a good mother.

Keep cool during the moments after hearing your child's yell and before seeing the injury. Don't mistake ketchup for blood and douse it with disinfectant.

Don't give your child the prescription. Pharmacists have wasted time trying to read kids' scribbling.

Don't let your child take more than five toys from the waiting room toy chest into the doctor's office.

When your daughter is home from school with a temperature, don't watch your soap opera without bringing her up to date.

You can't stand at the door of the doctor's waiting room and ask "Which ones are here for check-ups?" and "Which ones are here because you're sick?" so you'll know where to sit.

All I Want For Christmas
Is Her Two Front Teeth
To Come In Straight

You must be prepared to hear this news:
"Your daughter will have to wear braces,
Unless you move to Africa
Where veils cover women's faces."

A child is a gift from God.

They say, "Never look a gift horse in the mouth," but do look your gift child in the mouth to see if she needs orthodontic work.

There should be more variables in mouths so orthodontia wouldn't be needed as often as it is.

Haven't you ever wondered when the first braces were used, and when the percentage of children wearing them went up to 99%?

"Get rid of wrinkles without surgery!" is often advertised, but never is getting teeth straight without braces offered. Metal must be used to pull teeth aside so the others will have needed space.

When a baby puts his thumb in his mouth and stops crying, don't enjoy the peace. Worry about protruding teeth. Pull the thumb out, and tell yourself you are earning money by listening to crying.

Form a vigilante committee of your husband, babysitters, grandparents, brothers, sisters, aunts, uncles and friends to stop thumb-sucking.

Orthodontists are heroes. They make a better world. Because of them, millions more people smile.

If you are a good mother, you will do anything it takes to have your daughter smile without being self-conscious.

You can't tell her to go around with gloomy people, or only watch the all-news channel.

31

No child ever uses hand-me-down braces

A husband feels the burden of the budget keenly, and will often balk at orthodontic work.

The following are a few statements by fathers:

"She'll work on her personality more if she has crooked teeth."

"Next, mother elephants will be getting their offsprings' tusks straightened."

"Well, make the appointment. Maybe they'll straighten out themselves beforehand and you can cancel."

"Why can't she wear her brother's old braces?"

He might say, "Let her get a rich husband and he can pay for it," and you know she is not apt to get a rich husband if she doesn't have straight teeth.

Show your child "before" and "after" pictures of other orthodontia patients so she will be eager to wear braces. If you have to bribe your child to go to each appointment, it will add to the expense.

The cost is considerable. The money that you save on caramels for her doesn't make a dent.

You must see it through. You can't say, "Your father's hours have been cut, and you have to drop out of orthodontia." Third mortgages are not unheard of during this procedure.

With all this money put into straightening teeth, you must make sure proper care is given them. One mother said her son brushed so seldom that she checked to see if there were an expiration date on the toothpaste tube.

The following list offers a few suggestions to help insure that the beautiful teeth last:

Set the table with a toothbrush and dental floss next to the silverware.

Wear a THANK YOU FOR BRUSHING pin.

Call the Water Department to make sure the fluoride level is what it should be.

Promote peace among your children so he doesn't get punched in the mouth.

If she goes into modeling and her smile becomes her fortune, there's a chance she will think about reimbursing you for her orthodontia.

Mothers Are Dirt Busters

Wouldn't it be wonderful,
If when you bathed them after play,
Kids were like a carpet,
And there were dirt-resistant spray?

What child has ever said, "We're getting low on soap?"
There has never been one, which means it is a struggle to get your child to bathe.

However, part of the maintenance of a child from the minute he is born is the bath.

Even though bathing was part of the Infant Hygiene course you took in high school, and you passed, do not be confident. Squirming, stiffening, and screaming are the chief problems, and a doll doesn't do any of that.

You always hear mothers saying, "I gave the baby his bath," as if it is a foregone conclusion that a baby is bathed every single day.

Even in yesteryear, the baby wasn't one of the family members who received a bath only on Saturday night. Each morning at 10 A.M. the oven door would be opened so the heat would keep the baby warm while he was unclothed for bath time.

It is not necessary to give the baby a bath very day.

You do "spot-bathing" each time you feed him or change him. Unless the person holding the baby has greasy hands, the baby won't get dirty.

Your baby isn't going to say to someone, "My mother didn't bathe me today."

It is harder to accomplish the bath when the child is ambulatory. You must then round him up. No matter how filthy he gets, he will not turn himself in.

If you live in a new development where the lawns and sidewalks are under construction, the dirt will be multiplied. By nightfall, your child will look like a miniature bum.

Dragging a child with planted feet to the bathtub is not

easy, but it has to be done. Dirt cannot be erased. It cannot be vacuumed.

When you use a wet wipe, the child is willing to consider that a bath.

Don't let him tell you, "Real men don't bathe."

There is no back door in the bathroom, so once you get him in there, he is trapped.

You must remember that a kid is not "bad" because he is dirty and doesn't want a bath. Therefore, when you are bathing him, attack the dirt and not the child.

There is the ordinary bath, and then there is the "first-day-of-school-bath," the "doctor's examination bath," the "visiting your mother-in-law bath," and the "photograph bath." The latter ones take longer.

A responsible parent gives as thorough a bath in the winter as in the summer, even though not as much of the body shows in the winter.

Following are some tips to help you with bath duty:

> While the purpose of the bath is to get dirt off, try to make the child think the bath is time to have fun.
>
> Wear an Admiral's cap while you bathe him and sing, "Anchors Away."
>
> Give your daughter a wooden spoon as an oar, and she can pretend to paddle.
>
> Stuffed animals should not be used as bathtub toys.
>
> Keep the child as clean as possible. For example, serve cold cuts instead of barbecues.
>
> Wear waterproof attire. It is impossible to jump out of the way from a kneeling position.
>
> Even if you have a ceiling fan, you still have to towel dry the child.
>
> Should you use the same bath water for two children, bathe the cleaner one first.

Certain toys cannot be bathed

A clean child is necessary for you to have the reputation of being a good mother. Have excuses for missed dirt, such as, "He has an ear problem, so I can't thoroughly scrub his ears."

There's A Spill In
Aisle 2, 3, 4, 5, and 6

When shopping with kids who are wild,
There is one thing that is really great --
The clerk never bothers to check
A coupon's expiration date!

When you have borrowed food items from neighbors more than three times, it is time to go grocery shopping.

Since your grocery expense is huge, you will not want to add the price of a baby sitter to your food costs, so you will probably take your children along with you to the supermarket.

Children don't understand that when you are grocery shopping, you must consider economy, nutrition, value and easy preparation. Therefore, the time drags for them and they are very apt to misbehave.

Young ones can wipe out the supply of an employee giving food samples in minutes. If you ask toddlers to get you a can of something, they will most likely take it from the bottom of a stack. They will run around, and they will make noise.

You would think that store personnel watching the theft monitor would occasionally notice what a bad time you're having and offer to help you, but this never happens.

It is wise to have Scotch tape with you to repair the items your children tear open.

Here are some shopping-with-children suggestions:

Make two lists -- one list of the items you want and one list of threats to make if your children misbehave.

Bring along a play phone. Your child will feel like a big shot, having a cart phone.

Shopping is boring for children

Tell your son it's not polite to look in other people's carts. He'll want what is in there.

Make a game of counting how many times your daughter says, "I don't like that kind."

Shop during nap time. A roll of paper toweling can be used for a pillow.

If one child hits another, put one of your frozen items on the bruise.

Notice what shoppers with well-behaved children have in their carts.

There are certain things to avoid while getting provisions for the family:

Don't wait for a clerk to go and get you an item that isn't on the shelf. Go without. Your child will not stand still beside you until the clerk returns.

Don't ask the lady who is giving out samples to watch your children while you shop, no matter how grandmotherly she looks.

Don't let your children know that you are dieting. They'll constantly be saying, "You're not supposed to eat that."

Don't give a child your car keys to play with. It will make clerks nervous, thinking that you may not be able to leave.

Don't go down the pet food aisle if you don't have a pet. Your children will start begging for one.

Your child's last disturbing act will probably be to bump your arm when you are writing the check.

Get Your Mind Out Of The Clutter

Kids won't help with cleaning
If you grab them by their collars.
Say, "Maybe you will find a comic book
That's worth a thousand dollars."

Since the day you came home from the hospital with the first child, your home probably has had a case of severe messiness.

It appears like a garage sale moved into the house. Items are not only in disarray, but they look like they have been dismantled.

All mothers go through stages before they adjust to a messy house. First, there will be denial, then anger, and finally acceptance.

You will eventually decide that you will simply call a cleaning service when the last child moves out.

You can't get your children to assist you in your goal of having a neat house. Your arguments will hold no weight.

Telling them, "If anyone stops in, they'll think we're slobs," will do no good. They will just say, "You're being paranoid." When it comes to cleaning, children do not want to become involved. They think the only purpose of the broom closet is to play hide and seek.

One child sent his chore list to his grandmother for sympathy. Another child used her allowance to pay a friend to do the chores she was assigned.

Kids are good at coming up with excuses for not helping. The following are a few examples:

"If I'm vacuuming, I won't be able to hear the phone."

"Cleaning chemicals burn my eyes."

"I have scrubber's elbow."

Even though you tell your child that his room is part of

the house and you want it neat, he will feel no obligation to clean it. That is why doors are so precious. Let them do their thing.

So you will know that you're not alone in having children with messy rooms, the following are some reported statements by mothers:

"I was encouraged when she took eight dust cloths to her room, but she tied them together and escaped out the window."

"He thinks hangers are only for opening locked car doors."

"She stopped to use an emery board on her nails ten times while she was cleaning."

"You wouldn't think dust could settle the way his room shakes from his music."

"There are even clothes thrown on top of the canopy over her bed."

"He wants a mirrored ceiling so he can locate lost items."

One tip that could help -- Let him pick out the carpet for his room. There is a chance he'll keep the floor picked up so it will show.

While you can never expect children to volunteer to help you, or to put things back, there are some actions that can help the neat house cause.

Be careful not to bring one more thing into the house. Do not make a deposit at a bank that gives a blanket, toaster, or stuffed animal for doing so.

Encourage your children to have friendships with children whose homes are spic and span.

Tell them their dolls and toy soldiers have a curfew. They have to be in the toy box by 7:00 P.M.

*Tell them their dolls and toy soldiers have curfew --
they have to be in the toy box by 7:00 P.M.*

Make them name tags as if they are a professional cleaning service.

Put balloons on the vacuum sweeper.

Print signs with their names on them and paint diagonal lines on the floor of the garage. It will make them feel important to have designated parking spaces for their tricycles and bicycles.

Provide music, such as "Whistle While You Work," "This is the Way we Scrub the House," or Rocky's theme song.

Gold stars do not work as well as gold coins.

Putting off housework until the kids grow up is not the answer. Tricking people into thinking you are a better housekeeper than you are, is. The following are a few ideas:

Put a lemon in a bowl of fruit. It smells like you've been dusting.

Leave the doors and windows open. People might think that the dust just blew in.

Put a decal on your glass patio door. It will make it seem that you keep it so clean there is danger of someone trying to walk through it.

Vacuum your throw rugs before you shake them outside.

Say that the dust on the top of your grandfather clock is there to represent gray hair.

Leave a boarding pass in sight. It gives the impression you have been traveling and weren't home to clean.

If you have a dirty sofa pillow, throw it on the floor when the doorbell rings. People will assume it belongs to a cat or dog.

With children, you can expect that your carpet will be soiled. When someone comes, yell upstairs, "Who's tracking?"

Be sure you don't take pictures inside the house to send to your mother-in-law.

Their Temperatures Never Go Above 98.6 and Their Test Scores Never Go Below

Her kids are bathed and asleep
For a treat she's baked cinnamon twist --
No wonder numerous sitters ask,
"May I please be on your list?"

It seems like some mothers are mistake-proof.

They are so far ahead of the average mother that they are demoralizing.

You can't say to Super Mom, "You are making me miserable. Would you mind doing some flubbing up?" She would only deny her perfection.

Here are a few annoying actions of a Super Mom:

She comes home from the hospital wearing Size 3 jeans.

She writes all her children's excuses in calligraphy.

She never has a prescription in the medicine cabinet that is over a month old.

She warms Band-Aids before she puts them on her children.

She knows the exact minute when she should change the smoke alarm batteries, and does it.

She synchronizes her watch with her baby sitter's and is never one minute late.

She has her children attach deposit slips to the money that they drop into their piggy banks, so they will be prepared for real banking.

She identifies birds and trees for the children in the carpool.

46

***Super Moms are not admired as much
as they think they are***

47

Super Mom's children are equally detrimental to an average mother's morale. Here are some symptoms of the "perfect child" of the "perfect mother."

He has never put anything except food in his mouth.

She never asks her grandparents, "What did you bring me?"

She is trying to get in the Guiness Book of Records for getting the most gold stars.

He saves 99% of the money he gets for delivering newspapers for his college education.

She asks, "Is there a Page Two on my chore list?"

He is thrilled when he sees you visiting his school.

She always chooses a baked potato instead of french fries in a restaurant.

He has a standing appointment for a haircut.

She has college recruiters after her when she is in third grade.

He rotates the tires on his tricycle.

She has never lost a mitten.

He always returns the car with a full tank of gas.

While you must accept the fact you will never be Super Mom, there are things you can do that will create the illusion that you are:

Have bookshelves built into the headboard of your baby's bed.

Smudge food on your child's flash cards. It will look to the teacher as though you left your cooking to help your son with his homework.

Send items for Show and Tell in an oatmeal box.

If you ever do give your child a hot breakfast and he gets egg or oatmeal on his face, leave it.

Even though your kids only eat junk food, leave a banana peel or orange skin lying in the toy room.

Leave a little girl's apron with flour on it in plain sight. It will give the impression that you are teaching your daughter to bake.

Say, "I enjoy having my children underfoot," not letting it be known that you mean, "I like having them play in the basement."

Always leave teachers' conferences smiling.

You should not let yourself feel too much pressure. Cases of Super Moms with perfect children are extremely rare.

There Is No Substitute for Bed

When he calls out to you for water,
You tell him no child died of thirst.
He will not be placated --
He'll say, "I could be the first."

Telling a two-year-old that she will have bags under her eyes in the morning if she doesn't get to sleep will not help you in the all-important quest of securing peace and quiet.

When you have spent the day being a mother, the desire to have a little childless time in the evening is easily understood. However, it is not always easily achieved.

In one way, children are all the same. They resist going to bed.

An adult is wise enough to think of sleep as body repair, but a child thinks of it as punishment. He considers it detention.

Your daughter always pleads that she is not tired. Does she think you are going to say, "Oh, well then, forget it?"

Your son either has such a passion for life that he doesn't want the day to end, or the little devil wants to keep bugging you.

However you view it, you want him in bed, so it is worth putting some thought into getting him there.

Arguments get silly:

"You won't grow if you don't get sleep."

"I'll grow anyhow."

"No, you won't."

"Yes, I will."

"No, you won't."

"Yes, I will."

If you say, "Let's get ready for bed," it sounds like you're going to bed, too, and he'll make a fuss when he finds out you aren't.

Bedtime sounds better to the mother than to the child

Children have many stalling strategies, such as:

"That nice man on TV told me to keep watching."

"I have to rotate the tires on my tricycle."

Nothing is too much trouble in getting children to slumberland:

Let her pack a suitcase as if she's staying overnight at a motel.

Get him a beeper for his pajamas, and tell him if he goes to bed, he can beep you if he needs anything.

Tell her you'll go out and buy the cereal of her choice to have in the morning.

There should be a computer program for getting children to bed.

Here are some suggestions to help get your cherubs to toddle off:

Hire a baby sitter and hang around to see how she does it.

Keep the drapes drawn all day so you can lie about bedtime.

Have a sleepathon. Tell the kids you'll give them a penny for every minute they sleep.

Tell your children their stuffed animals are lonesome for them.

Make up jingles about bed and sing them:

"Mr. Bed is a wonderful friend--

He makes it fun to see the day end."

"Violets are blue, roses are red.

I love Mommy, Daddy and bed."

Keeping children in bed is as challenging as getting them there.

Here are some suggestions to help you accomplish this miraculous feat:

> Learn to lip read so you can turn off the sound on the TV.
>
> Only do a bed check if you are absolutely sure the children are asleep.
>
> Don't let your daughter look at a catalogue. She'll keep getting out of bed to show you the things she wants.

If one child wants the light on and one wants it off, leave it on and put sunglasses on the other one.

Don't Punish for Spilled Milk --
Do Punish for Thrown Milk

You must keep your child from wrong --
If it's his biting everyrone's afraid of
Don't use the "Bite-'em-back" cure.
Say, "Spinach is what people are made of."

You cannot divorce your children. You must shape them up so that they are fit to live with.

However, there is an advantage to dealing with a child over a husband. You can use discipline.

The evolution of discipline is baffling. A mother is supposed to feel that quiet time is just as effective as a strap in the woodshed.

You can't have your child get a physical exam to see if it's okay to spank him. Spanking is out.

But no punishment has ever been guaranteed.

It is fun to show a child love by buying him toys, but it is miserable to show love by punishing.

Misbehavior can be handled in many different ways, but it cannot be ignored. You must make sure your child is not "discipline-denied."

The importance of looking at your child objectively cannot be stressed enough. Many parents fail to do this.

Here are a few signals that your child is less than perfect:

He gets extra credit for being absent.

Neighbors always have their cement poured while your family is on vacation.

You often find the phone off the hook and the mailbox in his room.

Your babysitter tells you she is retiring after sitting for you once.

It's hard to find out everyone doesn't appreciate
your children

Remember, the child who has done something wrong wants to be punished. However, don't wait until he puts his desire into words to punish.

The following are some suggestions to help you discipline effectively:

Eat garlic before you deliver a lecture to your son. He will agree with you a lot sooner.

Add one more chore to her chore list. If you can't think of one, take one from your husband's chore list.

You can't say, "Remain in your room for two hours," and then leave the house. You have to stay on duty.

The time just flies for you during their "time-outs." You'll say, "It can't be two hours already." You had better use a timer.

Make him add, subtract, multiply and divide for a week without a computer.

Have her do several hours of household service, such as weeding the garden, scrubbing the bathtub, etc. Misdeeds won't be so hard to take if you know the misbehaving will eventually benefit you.

Make him listen to a tape of 1940's music.

Have her stand, rather than sit, during disciplinary quiet time. Otherwise she may blame you later for "quiet-time spread."

Tell him he has to get rid of the next door-to-door salesman.

Discipline should be recognized as punishment. If you order her to sit in a chair, it shouldn't be a Lazy-Boy.

Threaten to sew up the holes in his jeans.

There are many things, other than disciplining, that you

can do if you have a mischievous child:

> Get outdoor pets, such as rabbits or homing pigeons, to keep him outside more.

> Volunteer to be on telephone committees so teachers can't get through to you.

> Go to PTA meetings. You may get the school to lengthen the school day.

> Tell your child to use an alias if he ever writes his name in wet cement.

In the process of making your child a good adult, there are a few things it is best not to do:

> If he neglects to feed the dog, don't neglect to feed him.

> Don't try to make her better by telling people about her crimes. Her friends won't care, and her grandparents won't believe it.

> Don't postpone punishment by saying, "Wait until your father gets home," or, if you are a single parent, "Wait until I get you a father."

The discipline works better if you have the backing of the rest of the household -- your husband and the other children. It would be ideal if the dog growled and bared his teeth.

Birthday Parties
Should Be Considered
Unlawful Assemblages

The party time you spend
With these noisy little creatures
Makes you well aware
Of the gratitude owed teachers!

The best mother gives the child a birthday party at home rather than at a movie theater, bowling alley, or pizza parlor, even though she could be considered to be a masochist.

A birthday party is an event where a kid who is always late for school shows up an hour early, and where the kid who is ordinarily bashful shouts at the top of his lungs.

Birthday parties are extremely detrimental to your house. If you are planning on redecorating, you should have the party beforehand, even if it is three months ahead of the child's birthday.

There are a few things you should do before the actual event:

Get a stress test.

Have prospective guests for dinner one at a time -- like an audition.

Plan games. You can't say to five-year-olds, "Just mingle."

Tell your child not to say, "I already have one of these."

Make up 10 stanzas of HAPPY BIRTHDAY.

Find someone who hauls away debris.

Even if you print on the invitations that the party will be a "liver supper," every kid you invite will show up. In fact, if you send out 10 invitations, you shouldn't be surprised if 50 kids arrive.

Give a birthday party during your lunch hour

At an adult party, a guest is apt to put a lampshade on his head. At a kids' party, a guest is apt to break a lamp. It will be a wild and hectic time, and you will constantly be looking at your watch, wishing for the party to end.

The following are some suggestions that will help make the party easier on you:

Don't blow up the balloons before hand. Let the kids do it, and it will sap some of their energy.

Like lawyers, mothers dress their children in clothes that make them look innocent. Don't fall for that. Keep your eye on each and every one of them.

Let your answering machine take care of phone calls. Distractions can lead to disasters.

If your child says she can't invite certain kids to her party because they are not speaking to each other, invite them anyway. It could result in a quieter party.

Provide a new handkerchief for Blindman's Bluff. Some kid might point out that her dad's handkerchiefs are a lot whiter.

Use TV language. Say, "If you don't pipe down, the cops'll bust us."

Have a prize for everyone. Good losers are nonexistent.

Say, "We are now going to play a game called "Clean Up."

Hosting a birthday party is one of the most courageous acts a mother ever performs. However, even heroes get cowardly thoughts.

The following are some desperate moves that might occur to you to make, but you must resist:

Before you send out the invitations, go to the school and check each child's grade in conduct.

Write the word "sharp" on the invitations after the party's ending time.

Say, "I just received a bomb threat. You'll have to play outside."

Send the kids home from a slumber party at midnight because it is no longer your child's birthday.

Have your child open the presents immediately so you can be nicer to the ones who give the most expensive presents.

Give them all fortune cookies containing fortunes that read, "You will only be happy in your own home."

It helps to write about it in your diary.

Can You Be Arrested For Forging a Thank You Note?

They receive many a gift
About which they're ecstatic,
But they delay writing "Thank You"
'Til the gift's in the attic.

Do you hope your child will never receive another gift? If so, it is no doubt because of the difficulty you have in getting your child to write a thank-you note.

A lot of conversation will take place between you and your child about his need to express his gratitude for a present.

The following are some typical statements of children:

"Can't I just write one big thank you when I turn 18?"

"I wish I had been born on February 29."

"I know Aunt Emma got the present on sale. Can I write a real short note?"

"Now I know why it's better to give than to receive."

Some typical statements of mothers on the subject:

"No, you can't call Grandma collect and say, "Thank you."

"If you can't spell generous, use kind."

"No, Aunt Grace won't write you a thank-you note for your thank-you note."

Your offspring will give all kinds of excuses for not writing a thank-you, such as, "I don't want to be the cause of Grandma having to hunt for her glasses."

When you meet the giver of the gift, you will feel compelled to explain why she hasn't been thanked.

You can't blame slow mail if more than a month has elapsed.

The following list offers a few suggestions of things to say that will make **you** feel better, even if they won't necessarily make the donor think more kindly of your child:

> "Tyler had your thank-you note in his pocket, and I washed his jeans."

> "As soon as Emily learns to spell better, she's going to write you."

> "Adam's note to you is in its final draft."

> "You'll be getting your thank-you as soon as that clumsy cast gets off."

Only a very rude person would respond, "Are you sure he isn't waiting for a stamp with his head on it to be issued?"

Here are some suggestions to help your child get on with the task of note-writing:

> Have your child buy a toy with his monetary gift, and don't let him play with it until he has written a thank-you note.

> Give her paper, pen and a list of gushy adjectives.

> Make him buy his own stamps, and tell him that the price of stamps is going up.

> Tell her to write, "Write thank-you notes," on her list of things to do. If she won't make a list of things to do, you make a list and write on it, "hound Jennifer to write her thank-you's"

Here are a few more hints about thank-you notes:

> Be sure the note you wrote for your child to copy does not accidentally get placed in the envelope along with his note.

Parents feel responsible for their children's thank-you's

Don't send a note in advance that says, "Thank-you note will be forthcoming."

Don't use calligraphy if you are forging the note.

If your prodding fails, have a thank-you published in the newspaper.

One mother had her child so well-trained to write thank-you's that when he shoplifted some bubble gum, he wrote a thank-you letter to the grocer and was thereby caught.

No, We Can't Take
The Tree House With Us

Don't expect for a minute
It will ward off a sob,
If you say, "Children, dear,
It is a much better job."

Transfers aren't only given to the childless, but it takes real courage to tell your kids that you will be moving.

A move across the city can be just as traumatic as a move across the country.

Your children are apt to throw eggs at your FOR SALE sign.

You don't want your children to be so unpleasant that they have no friends, but that would be helpful when you are forced to move.

It is good if each child has a pen pal. Then he or she will still have that friend after the move.

Kids having to move act like they are being kidnapped — and they would like you to receive the same punishment that kidnappers get.

While you can't expect them to say, "Faster! Faster!" on the way to the new house, you **can** do certain things to achieve some degree of acceptance.

The following are a few suggestions:

> Find a realtor who pledges to convince your children that moving is a good idea.
>
> Say, "Daddy is going to get a raise, and that means you will get a raise in your allowance, but we will have to move to get those raises."
>
> Get an 800 number so your children's friends can call them, free.

*Do anything you can think
of to help them adjust to moving*

Rent Barney or a current popular character and ask new neighbors to pretend it lives with them.

Say, "You can have a dog." This will be effective if you don't have one. It won't work to say, "You can have another dog."

Exaggerate. Tell them, "There's going to be a swing set in the back yard, and maybe even a roller coaster."

Even if you're moving from Wisconsin to Illinois, say that you'll be going by way of Disney World.

Tell your girls that the lighting in the new house makes the mirrors more flattering.

Give a prize to the one who collects the most boxes for the move.

Say, "Maybe your report cards will get lost in the mail when they are forwarded."

Tell them, "This house is on the route of an ice cream truck."

Make WELCOME banners for their rooms.

Tell one child that she can ride up front with the movers.

Tell one child he can be the door opener for the movers.

Make a list of advantages of the new location, such as "there are five more stores in that mall," and "the new cable TV company gets six more channels . . ."

Here are a couple of no-no's to observe:

Don't wait until the movers get to your house to tell the children you are moving.

Don't say, "Daddy's boss is the one who is doing this. He's the one to whom you should say, 'I hate you!'

Is There A Camp Counselor
In The House?

Making your child blow up his air mattress
Could cause the kid to pout,
But he'll be less trouble after that,
Because he'll be worn out.

Do you hate camping so much that the only place you want to pitch the tent is through the department store window where you bought it?

You better reconsider. Children take their time growing up, and camping can make the time pass more quickly.

There are pleasant aspects of camping -- beautiful views, eating food cooked over an open fire, and having the moon and stars overhead.

Other good things about camping:

There are no people to tip.

Kids can't slam a tent door.

You don't have to vacuum spills.

Your reflection in the lake is flattering.

If your kids get in fights with other kids, they won't live by you for long.

But even if you talk yourself into thinking that camping is great, you should not expect perfect bliss.

Views do not mean as much to children as they should. Almost no time is spent oohing and aahing.

Camping changes your children's regular routine, and this could tend to make them lean toward being unmanageable. Casual living can lead to mischief.

Also, your children will often complain about what they are missing on TV. Bringing along the TV Guide so they can read a synopsis of their favorite programs won't help one bit.

69

You will have a stiff neck from looking at the sky to see if it is going to rain.

Statements during a camping expedition should include "Isn't it glorious?!" and "This is the way to live!"

However, samples of some more common statements are:

"I know you're never able to sleep with the light on, but I can't do anything about the stars."

"You are not going to sit in the car until we go home."

"There is no way a telephone can be installed at a campsite for a weekend."

Here are some suggestions that could make you a happy camper -- or at least a "happier camper."

Pick a good campsite. A good campsite is one that is within five minutes of a motel.

Take a direct route, rather than a scenic route, to the campground. It is easier to enjoy the scenery when the kids are out of the car.

If you run out of clean clothes for your children, put their dirty ones on inside out and say they dressed themselves.

Keep the food up high in the trees, out of reach of bears and kids.

Award the title of "Best Camper" and "Worst Camper."

Make your children keep their life jackets on at all times. This will protect them from their siblings' blows.

When getting sticks to roast marshmallows, find branches with lots of leaves. It will take more time to strip them.

There are some things you should **not** do in your quest for a happy camping experience:

Don't buy insect repellent for your children --
scratching keeps them busy

Don't camp in a valley. The echo will cause you to hear bad words twice.

Don't buy insect repellent for your children. Scratching will keep them busy.

Don't let your son bring his amplifiers for around-the-campfire singing.

Don't try to teach anyone under two-years-old how to read a compass. Watch them so they don't wander away.

Don't let your children put a notice in the camp office, asking for a ride home.

Don't use every pan for tent drips. Save one or two for cooking.

Don't sing camp songs that are TV theme songs.

There is danger in having a car phone. Your husband could say he has been called to work and leave you alone with the kids.

Maxims Give Words
Maximum Strength

Socrates and Aristotle thought thoughts
That are well to bear in mind,
But a mother can surpass their gems,
Going through her daily grind.

You can go through motherhood more easily if facts are made catchy.

The following are 25 examples:

You must go the distance when you are raising children, and there is no finish line.

Peace is the absence of war and children.

Read to your children -- something besides the riot act.

Parents give their children the ammunition with which they shoot off their mouths.

Don't let the last pat on the back you give your child be for burping.

If you always give your child free rein, he won't know what you mean when you say, "Whoa!"

Behind every successful man is a mother who is emotionally and financially drained.

School is the place you send your kids to improve their minds so you won't lose yours.

A mother has to live down her kids living it up.

During the teen years, children put their parents on hold.

Imitation is the sincerest form of making fun of you.

Absence makes the school call you at work.

Motherhood is never finished.

A mother has a sixth sense that her kids don't have any.

Children today are creatures of grab it.

Kids think money grows on trees, and there is always a bumper crop.

If you continually harp, your kids will wish you were playing one.

A child wants your time, but even more he wants money from your Tyme.

A baseball diamond is a mother's best friend.

Your daughter is a built-in babysitter only until the boys notice she is "built."

Kids go from one phase right into another. They are never phased out.

As they grow up, you will wait up.

Raising a child means raising your voice.

Every man who has ever lived has made mistakes and has had a mother to excuse them.

"Mrs. Jones, Are You Listening? I Was Talking About Your Son's Attention Span."

"Your son draws funny pictures of me,"
Is the complaint you hear from the teacher.
"You just draw funny pictures of him"
Is not a solution that will reach her.

It is not a teacher's goal to spare the parent. Educators feel the mother and father should be informed of their children's mischievous acts. This is done via teachers' conferences.

No matter how successful you are in the business world, this is not a case of saying, "My people will call your people." You must sit in that chair facing the teacher and listen to what she has to say.

The following are some signs that the meeting might not go well:

You find your car keys hidden in a drawer in your son's room.

You are scheduled for two different sessions.

The teacher asks to see both parents.

The principal is sitting in on the conference.

Your aim should be to make school better for your child because of the conference. There will also be the selfish aim of making the conference less miserable for you.

Here are a few suggestions that could help matters:

Ask the teacher what fragrance she is wearing. She'll either think you admire the way she smells, or that you are planing to give her a gift.

Buy the teacher a lottery ticket. There's a chance he or she could win and quit teaching.

76

The teacher says kinder things to a grandmother

Ooh and aah about the teacher's bulletin boards.

Go to the conference with an unruly toddler. The teacher will hurry.

Bring along your mother or mother-in-law. The teacher is apt to say less terrible things in front of a grandmother.

Have a box of tissues with you. It could make the teacher fear that you are going to cry

Try to get your child out of the conversation by asking the teacher about her vacation, where she went to college, etc.

Words can work magic in making the teacher say better things about your child than she had planned.

Here are a few bewitching statements to assure a positive conference atmosphere:

"You are the prettiest and smartest teacher Kristen has ever had."

"Could we discuss this over a prime rib dinner at my house?"

"When you smile your dimples show."

"I'm not a single parent, so you would make two people happy if you give a good report."

"Remember that note you sent home with her? She cut off your signature and put it among her auto graphs."

On the other hand, here are a few no-no's for conference time:

Don't tell the teacher the nickname the kids have for him.

Don't deny anything the teacher says about your child. She can probably verify her accusations with the substitute teachers.

Don't yawn while the teacher is talking, even though the conference is at the end of the day.

Don't pick up two erasers and hold them over your ears.

Don't slam the door on your way out.

Here are some statements that you would be better off **not** making:

"Here's a new red pen. I'm sure you've worn yours out."

"Hasn't anyone ever told you that if you can't say anything good about somebody, you shouldn't say anything?"

"He'll have to change his attitude?! How about **you** changing **your** attitude?"

"Could we take a break and start in again in about ten minutes?"

And remember, it's always tacky to bring up the Christmas gift that your child gave her.

Surly to Bed and
Surly to Rise

She is no longer pleased with Mother;
She yearns for her removal.
But somehow she must face the fact:
You can't take mothers on approval.

The good qualities your child has are hidden. The years of adolescence have arrived.

At 12-years-old, your child loves you for the dedicated, unselfish person you are. You are admired.

Suddenly overnight, the way you lick a stamp is now disgusting to your 13-year-old.

While adolescents are gaining their individuality, it is impossible to be continuously at peace with them. They are leaving childhood and entering adulthood, and unpleasantness is part of the process.

If your teens don't become ornery, they will never be capable of making decisions. When they are 50, they will go through a cafeteria line and end up with only a napkin and silverware.

If you have several teen-agers, they will all agree that you need a complete make-over.

It is surprising that they don't break one another's ribs with their constant elbowing whenever you are talking.

These are trying years. It is best not to diet or give up smoking during this time. You will need all of the gratification you can get!

You didn't ask for the role of the "heavy," but you have it. When your husband says, "Do I have to separate you two again?!" it is demeaning. But this must be endured.

"Could I have one day a week off from having my life made miserable?" is a futile request.

Following are a few signals that will let you know that your child has reached adolescence.

Bonding between mother and daughter is difficult.

When he is with you in a restaurant, your son hangs onto the menu so he can cover his face with it when someone he knows walks in.

Your daughter refuses to dust because she didn't put the dust there.

You have conversations such as:

Son: "What are we having for lunch?"

Mother: "Chili" (putting it into bowl for him)

Son: "I don't like chili." (Mother puts a little more into bowl)

Son: "I said I don't like chili." (Mother stops putting chili into bowl)

Son: "Is that all I get?!"

Your daughter is starting to save her money for blue contact lenses, because she inherited your brown eyes.

Trying to be buddy-buddy, only makes you seem more of a fuddy-duddy.

However, there are some things you **can** do during this miserable time that might help:

Read the book WHEN BAD THINGS HAPPEN TO GOOD PEOPLE.

Say over and over, "I am a good person. I am an intelligent person. I am a fair person."

Tell yourself, "I'm doing good mothering. She isn't doing good daughtering."

Since every order you give has to be negotiated, talk to someone who negotiates union contracts.

Studies prove that children who wear school uniforms behave better. If you child's school has uniforms insist he leave it on until he goes to bed.

Should you call home and your teen answers, ask her to turn on the answering machine. She is more apt to listen to the machine message than your words directly.

Don't let your son wear his earphones during Jeopardy. You want him to know how many answers you get.

Ask a friend to tell your daughter that she has a beautiful smile.

Have your ophthalmologist tell your son that it is dangerous to roll his eyes heavenward.

Get your dog to like you. There is a chance your teen may respect the dog's opinion.

Remember, during this time you win none and <u>really lose</u> others.

They Are Not Elated
About Being Related

"Straighten up! Walk faster!
Speak louder! Must you mumble?"
They certainly help you to achieve
The virtue of being humble.

The days of your child running after you and yelling, "Wait up, Mom," are gone.

No matter how good you look, what a fine house you have, what a sporty car you drive, how successful you are in the business world, when your child becomes an adolescent, she will be embarrassed by you.

Your son is not relaxed one minute when he is with you.

You couldn't have a sergeant in basic training be pickier. Your teen notices everything you do wrong. You are under constant inspection.

Your daughter offers you a Vitamin C tablet because your sneeze embarrasses her.

If you were your son's attorney, he wouldn't want you to say anything to defend him.

Your daughter is acutely aware of any grammatical errors or utensil violations.

Your son edits the school excuses you write for him.

It is not hostility. It is pure embarrassment.

Thoughtless people will say your daughter looks like you. They do not realize how you will suffer later because of her carrying on at home when she is told this.

You must hang onto little things, like your son asking, "Where were you?" if you weren't home when he got there. It is all the endorsement you are going to get.

Here are some tip-offs that your child is embarrassed by you:

He says, "Don't hail a cab, Mom, I'll do it."

84

A mother can't be sensitive.

You attend a school event, and your daughter insists that if you wear a name tag, it will ruin your dress.

Your son is walking with you, but as friends approach, he stoops to tie his shoe lace, and he is wearing loafers.

While walking with your daughter, she puts her coat over her head, and it's not raining.

You get to school to chaperone a dance, and your son says to you, "Wait in the car, and I'll get you if anything bad happens."

Your daughter asks you to visit her campus during spring break.

A mother is not supposed to compare her child to another child. It follows that a child should not compare his mother to another mother.

Do You Need A New Mirror?

It's common for teen-agers
To look a fright.
It would seem to rule out
Love at first sight.

Kids wear very strange clothes and get very strange haircuts.

Perhaps it can be compared to hitting a spoon against a glass and saying, "Ladies and Gentlemen! May I please have your attention?!"

Hair and clothes are most destructive forces in a child's appearance.

When you think he can't look worse, somehow he manages to do so.

Each time she comes in with packages, you optimistically hope they contain decent clothes. Never! If they were free, they would be overpriced.

In the summer, he wears three layers. In the winter, he wears tank tops, shorts and thongs.

She is not attired. She is decorated.

There are side effects to this hair and these clothes. They are moodiness and disrespect.

But they are not going to say, "I'm going to go shopping" or "I'm going to the barber shop. Want to come along?" You must learn to co-exist.

The following are a few suggestions to help you endure your teenager's appearance:

Lower your standards of grooming.

Don't compare him to young men you see at airports. Compare him only to kids you see on campuses.

Suggest she put her clothes on layaway. There's a chance she might change her mind before it's time to get them.

At least they won't be mugged for their clothes

Present him with a T-shirt that reads, "I HAVE GOOD CLOTHES IN MY CLOSET."

Look at her often when she is in bed covered with a quilt.

Since it takes a long time for a young man to get beard bored, the following are a few suggestions to help in getting him to shave.

Serve foods like spaghetti and barbecued ribs that are hard to get out of his beard.

Zip his jacket up so his beard gets caught.

Buy him a carton of bubble gum. Multiple popped bubbles could do the trick.

The only place to look for a picture of a clean-shaven rock star is in Ripley's BELIEVE IT OR NOT.

Girls are also too pro-hair. One mother said to her daughter, "We spent $3,000 to have your teeth straightened, and we don't want them covered up by bangs."

He doesn't seem to care how people view him.

If only his dog would refuse to let him take him for a walk.

They Love the Telephone, So Why Can't They Call When They're Late?

If you have a teen,
Your phone's never free.
Don't send invitations
That say, "R.S.V.P."

The words most frequently spoken by parents are, "It's for you."

How many teen-agers were on the phone during the moon walk? I'm sure there were more phone talkers than television viewers.

Nothing is more important to an adolescent than using Alexander Graham Bell's invention. (It is said that Mr. Bell had second thoughts about his invention when his children became teen-agers.)

The same child who has been accused by his teacher of having a short attention span has a two-hour phone conversation.

Once in a while the telephone is out of order, and this is considered a great tragedy by the adolescent. When she picks up the receiver and says, "Dead?!" it couldn't be said in a more grief-stricken tone if a loved one were dead.

You have to use a pot holder to pick up the receiver when she is through.

There are many varieties of calls, none of which lasts less then 15 minutes.

Sometimes phone conversations consist only of listening to music. Some are Where, When and Wearing What calls. Many are so boring that you can't understand why your teens don't get drowsy and doze off.

It might help to know that all mothers suffer telephone problems. Many a mother feels like picketing her child on

Nothing means as much as the phone.

the phone.

If a lawyer asked a teen-age witness, "Where were you on the night of August 24th?" and the teen answered, "I was on the phone from 6:00 until midnight," people on the jury would believe it.

Following are some typical comments by mothers regarding the teen phone phobia:

> "She'll never let herself get arrested, because she knows she would be allowed only one phone call."

> "It really upsets me when she uses the low-cut 'Hell-o'."

> "He makes me feel like I'm eavesdropping when he calls the Telephone Time Lady."

> "When she makes a long-distance call, I set the egg timer by her and she yells, 'Your eggs are done,' and goes right on talking."

> "My son suggested getting a fluorescent phone in case the lights go out."

> "The single good thing about her being on the phone is that the bathroom is vacant."

The only time you have the phone to yourself is when the teen is away from home.

The phone situation will never be great, but there could be some improvements:

> The call-waiting signal could be a loud, continuous shriek that couldn't be ignored.

> There could be phones installed in school lockers to cut down on home phone use.

You can't tear gas your teen to get them off the phone, but some creative thinking should achieve this in a non-violent way:

Burn something so the smoke alarm goes off and they can't hear.

Point to the D and F on the phone dial to hint that they should get on their homework.

The only telephone rule you can make that **might** hold up is: "No calls from 3:00 to 4:00 A.M."

Never Having To Say You're Sorry
Means You Don't Have Children

If your child does something
That causes you shame,
Hope it happens before
They can publish his name.

One mother said she was not going to feel proud when her child accomplished something great, and then she wouldn't have to be ashamed when he did something bad.

It will not work this way for her. When a child gets into a scrape, the mother is humiliated and mortified -- feelings that make her utterly miserable.

Being embarrassed by offspring is common. One day a TV star is saying, "My series was picked up." the next day he is saying, "My son was picked up."

There could easily be more than one of your children involved in an unfortunate incident. Sibling loyalty is very strong.

Whether it's an arrest for battery, or for stealing a battery, you feel it is the worst crime that anyone's child has ever committed. All the positive thinking in the world won't make the pain disappear.

It's not fair that you have to prepare a defense the same as the child who committed the crime, but you do.

Kids come up with ridiculous excuses of why they did what they did. One boy who made it into the Circuit Court log said to his mother, "I realized what a modest person you are and knew how uncomfortable you were with being proud of me."

It is not wise to go around with friends whose children are in sharp contrast to yours. A better choice would be to be friends of a couple who has a lawyer on "speed dial" because of their son's scrapes with the law.

It is not wise to expect perfect children.

There are ways to help you get through this rocky period:

> Say 100 times, "I love my children unconditionally." Increase this to 500 times if the disgrace is really bad.
>
> Form a support group.
>
> Count all your loved ones who are dead and don't have to live through this.
>
> Count all your enemies who are dead and aren't here to gloat over this.
>
> Get out all the pictures, cards and gifts your child made at school in the primary grades, and look at them lovingly.
>
> Check into the age limit of joining the Peace Corps.
>
> Turn your son's photo face down in your wallet.
>
> Buy yourself something new to wear. If you are too embarrassed to leave the house, order it from a catalogue.
>
> Add up the amount of tax money you saved, taking your child as a deduction.
>
> Go to a therapist. He will give you someone else on whom to blame this dilemma.
>
> Remember all the times your son carried the groceries into the house for you.
>
> Threaten to make your child pay for your Prozac.

Ordinarily there are limits to what you can do to relieve an unpleasant situation. Not here. You will do almost **anything** that will help lift this heavy weight.

Here are a few extreme actions that could make you feel better:

> Write hate letters to couples who are childless.

Cancel your subscription to the newspaper that carried the article about your child's arrest.

Rip up letters from your child's Alma Mater asking for donations.

Never, ever, say, "Good! I'm glad!" when a friend calls and tells you that her son has been arrested.

They Take the Flight,
And You Experience
The Turbulence

"With the grandkids there, expenses rise,"
You can hear me growling.
One cost that is extremely high
Is the rolls of paper toweling.

When your last child is out of the house, it is not the end of children for you.

Your children will have children, and they will expect your help with these offsprings.

This "help" will not be summoned on an every-day basis, but often enough so that when you hear your child's or child-in-law's voice on the phone, your heart sinks.

Years ago there weren't credit cards, so couples didn't take extended vacations. Men went to conventions without their wives. Long-term baby sitting wasn't often required.

Today it is, and grandmothers are asked to perform this difficult task.

Even if you are a competitive person, you don't get a kick out of asking people, "What is the longest time you ever sat with your grandchildren?"

"Sitting" is not the enjoyable part of being a grandmother, but it isn't easy to get out of this task when you are called upon.

Your children are clever in the way they ask for your help. They are apt to say, "I know you can't get enough of your grandchildren."

You should not respond, "Yes, I can -- in about an hour. I don't need days of playing cards, pitching balls, listening to riddles and answering questions." You must try to be just as clever as your children:

When they give you your instructions, say, "Let's go through it again," five or six times. This may destroy their confidence in you.

Say, "No, I can't baby-sit because you didn't ask me first." There is always a chance they **didn't** ask you first.

Say, "I'm starting to forget things. I can't remember the rules I had for them last time, and if I change rules, it could do serious psychological damage."

Say, "They'll be spoiled when you get home. I can't say 'No'."

Usually it is better to baby-sit than to suffer the guilt you will feel after refusing.

If your children say, "We don't want to tear you out of your home," don't fall for it. The damage to your house could be extensive.

Tell them, "I had better baby-sit at **your** house because I have Christmas presents hidden all over mine."

Cancel all the appointments you have during your baby-sitting time. You don't want three women waiting at a bridge table, and you certainly don't want to antagonize your dentist.

You are better off if you face the fact that your precious grandchildren are regular kids. Do not fantasize.

For instance, here are some statements you will **never** hear:

"If it's too much trouble, Grandma, don't bother."

"You already told me that, Grandma, but it bears repeating."

"You don't have to give me my allowance. Money would cheapen our relationship."

Just get through the day, days, week or (God, forbid) weeks. Do not have goals.

Don't be surprised if your grandchild cries until the
parents give her the present they brought you

Don't try to add new items to their diets.

Don't try to make improvements in their characters.

Don't try to get them to floss.

Don't try to get them to start a savings account.

Don't try to get rid of the undesirables among their friends.

Even if your children and their spouses have never had one argument, tell yourself that your baby-sitting is saving their marriages.

To avoid having a child cry for his Mommy and Daddy, do not "airplane" food into his mouth. It will remind him of his parents taking off.

The following are some additional suggestions to help you during a long-term baby-sitting job:

Charge them every time they say, "Mommy lets us."

Use the grandchildren to your advantage. If a phone solicitor calls, say, "I've got someone here who wants to say, 'Hello',"

Every day, have the grandkids make a different WEL-COME HOME sign.

It is important that you do not let the grandchildren know that taking care of them is not pleasant for you.

Don't tie a yellow ribbon around a tree.

Don't keep setting the timer so you'll know another hour has passed.

Don't throw darts at the brochure of the resort where their parents are staying.

Regarding the parent's return:
Refrain from combing your hair the day they are ar-

riving home so you will look more harassed.

Don't strangle them with their flowered leis, even in jest.

If your children were in Las Vegas, check to see if they lost money so you can stock the house with groceries before you leave.

Don't be surprised if your grandchild cries until the parents give her the present they had bought for you.

Post Facts of Life

Children must be told
About the bird and bee,
But there are other truths
To learn at mother's knee.

Facts of life are told so children will know the results of sexual involvement.

However, the facts of life story ends with the birth of the baby.

The knowledge of what happens after having a baby should also be imparted.

The following are some post facts of life:

Your kids use language they never heard you use, although they tempt you to use it.

It is impossible to enjoy gossip about friends' children, because you know your own are apt to do worse.

The worry of receiving failure notices from your kids' teachers makes junk mail thrilling.

Life isn't fair. If life were fair, kids wouldn't be having their best times while parents are having their worst times.

Dirt never covers a child so completely that people can't recognize him as yours.

Unbreakable toys take longer to break.

Medicine is never flavored so well that a child takes it without protest.

No matter how hard you try, all you'll ever be to your adolescent is one-half of a set of bad parents.

A crying child can be heard over a parade band.

A crying child can be heard over a parade band

By the time you have learned to say, "No," to your child, he will have learned to say, "No" to you.

Letting a child go barefoot adds bath time.

If you forbid your kids to watch TV, they will pick up books more often, but often to throw at each other.

Kids' Senior Class parties go on until their college homecomings.

A good example of mixed emotions is hearing your son get home. You're happy he's home, but unhappy that his car makes that noise.

Children see to it that you get your money's worth out of tranquilizers.

When you get the last dish put away, someone will want ice cream.

Your son will discover his term paper is missing right after the garbage has been hauled away.

When you have fixed a meal with all four food groups, your kids will decide to eat with **their** groups.

During the few minutes you leave your toddler outside unattended, your mother-in-law will drive by.

A missing shoe will not show up until it is too small.